THE LITTLE BOOK OF
PROFANITIES

First published in 2020 by OH!
An Imprint of Welbeck Non-Fiction Limited,
part of Welbeck Publishing Group.
Based in London and Sydney.
www.welbeckpublishing.com

ISBN 978-1-91161-048-9

Compiled by: Malcolm Croft
Editorial: Lesley Leverne
Project manager: Russell Porter
Design: Tony Seddon
Production: Rachel Burgess

A CIP catalogue record for this book is available from the British Library

Printed in Dubai

10 9 8 7 6 5 4 3 2

Images: freepik.com

THE LITTLE BOOK OF
PROFANITIES

KNOW YOUR
SH*TS FROM YOUR F*CKS

CONTENTS

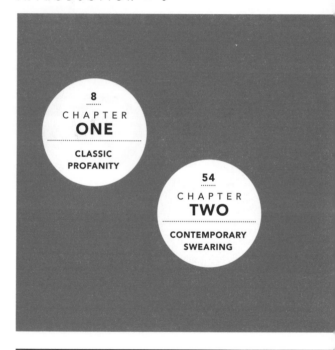

INTRODUCTION

There's nothing better than the *perfect* swear word. It's what makes talking to other twats so much more interesting. When you hear that pitch-perfect piece of profanity it can make your heart sing as if it were your new favourite song. And, like all things, variety is the spice of life. If you swear all the time it loses all impact and if you repeat the same curse *ad nauseam* swearing loses its joy. That's what this tiny tome is for: to proliferate your profanity. But not just turn you from a casual swearer to a compulsive one, no, but to make your cursing *better*, *funnier*, more, dare I say it, intelligent. For example, why call someone a *dick* (and you will, probably very soon) when you can call them a *choad*? How much more satisfying is that? Try that one for size. I promise you'll be back for seconds. (If only the same could be said for choads, poor things.)

Today, in this senseless and chaotic modern world, profanity remains as powerful as it is powerless. It only has meaning if you allow it to. As our societies have evolved over time, our curse word vocabularies have exploded beyond control. *Crikey*, *gadzooks* and *golly* have all gone the way of the dodo. And the reason is simple: survival of the fittest. They weren't good enough to survive. In the past 50 years alone, our vocabularies have detonated with new curse words. Creative compound swear words, or "franken-swears", such as spunktrumpet, shitgibbon, wankpuffin, etc, have surged in popularity thanks to the dawn and dominance of the Internet. Will they still be around in 100 years? Probably not, but they will be replaced by invective no doubt even more inventive. Because as society progresses, so does our swearing. But, anyway, enough of this bullshit. I'm off to delete my Internet search history and scrub my laptop out with hot soapy water, because in researching this book it's become full of the most despicable (and delicious) words known to modern humankind.

I hope you enjoy reading this book as much as I did writing it. And, if you don't, well, you can fuck the fuck off.

$#@!

CHAPTER
ONE

CLASSIC PROFANITY

"The sort of twee person who thinks swearing is in any way a sign of a lack of education or a lack of verbal interest is just a fucking lunatic."

Stephen Fry

Shit /schyt/

It happens

1. something, or someone, that's not considered good or helpful **2.** fecal matter **3.** a general term of abuse

The Swiss Army knife of swearing – helpful in all situations. Shit can be employed as an abstract exclamation ("Oh, shit!"), a declaration of poor quality ("That's shit!"), and faeces ("I've done a shit"). Paradoxically, it can also mean amazing ("That's *the* shit, right there!")

The word's etymology can be traced back to around AD 450, when **scite** (dung), **scitte** (diarrhoea) and **scitan** (to defecate) were all thrown about. Shit evolved a millennium later into **schitte** (excrement) and **shiten** (to defecate). The height of shit's early fame has been traced back to around 1500, when it was used to describe an obnoxious person, as in "Come back with my goat, you little shit!"

"Life is a crap carnival with shit prizes."
Stephen King

Scheisse (German) • Mierda (Spanish) • Merde (French) • Skit (Icelandic)

DON'T FORGET: crap, bullshit, horseshit, dogshit, pigshit, sheepshit

Fuck /fuhk/

75 per cent more sweary than any other leading profanity

1. to make love (aggressively) **2.** an exclamation of frustration or disdain

Some historians claim that the word was first recorded in 1310 with the gentleman "Roger Fuckbythenavel", who was summoned to court at the time for his love of ladies of the night. But, when a word is that satisfying to say, who the fuck cares where it came from?

"I couldn't give a flying fuck about the ..."

Fokken (Dutch) • Fanculo (Italian) • Tā mā de (Chinese) • Kuso (Japanese) • Sshi-bal (Korean) • Kurwa (Polish) • Oy, gevalt! (Yiddish) • Joder (Spanish) • Kut (Dutch)

Bastard /baa·stuhd/

Sounds better coming from the mouth of a tough-as-tits Northerner (bas-ted!) than a soft-as-shit Southerner (bar-stood)

1. an unpleasant person 2. something difficult to do 3. an illegitimate child

Illegitimate children can't catch a break. Just when they thought they'd been through enough, we go and call them bastards. The most famous bastard in recent times has been Jon "the bastard" Snow from *Games of Thrones*. And perhaps Nigel Farage. Further back in time, the word bastard sprang from the medieval Latin terms ***bastardus***, meaning "packsaddle". Whatever the bastard that is.

"My husband's a proper bastard." / "This jar is a right bastard to open."

Hùn zhàng (Chinese) • Jeot-gat-eun-nom (Korean) • Bastardo (Italian) • Cabra / Cabrão (Portuguese) though Desgraçado (Portuguese) is fun too!

Son of a Bitch /sohn·ova·bich/

A brother from another motherfucker

1. an unfriendly and unlikeable person **2.** an expression of disbelief and surprise

Son of a bitch was birthed from the phrase biche-sone ("slut's son") that was first recorded circa AD 1000. A bitch, originating from a female dog in heat, has long been used to derogatively describe women, itself traced back to ancient Greece and the use of the word "dog" as an insult.

"My mother never saw the irony in calling me a son of a bitch."
   Jack Nicholson

Ullu ka patha (Hindi) • Putain de salope (French: whore of a whore)

Fucker /fuhk·er/

Less familial than a motherfucker

1. an unfortunate situation **2.** an unfriendly person
3. someone who makes love aggressively

The act of being a "fucker" dates to the first person who a) fucked and b) gave a fuck – so let's blame Adam and Eve!

"This ski boot is an absolute fucker to get on."

Ficker (German) • Fecker (Irish) • Puto (Spanish)

Asshole /aas·howl/

The birthplace of shit

1. a lousy, lazy or loathsome individual **2.** the place where your poo comes from

A derivation of ye olde English **earsðerl**, and later, ***arce-hoole***. Asshole, or arsehole if you prefer, has been used to mean a contemptible person since the 1930s.

"Steve's an absolute asshole when he's been drinking."

Stronzo (Italian) • Rego do cu (Asscrack, Portuguese) • Malaka (Greek) • Je te pisse à la raie! (French: I piss on your asshole)

Crap /krap/

A shite so polite there's no need to wipe

1. an expression of mild annoyance **2.** something or someone that is rubbish **3.** an expression of nonsense

Crap is hardly considered the coolest swear word these days but its history is more than interesting enough for inclusion. The derives from farming language and the Old Dutch word ***krappen*** meaning "to cut off, pluck off" and the Latin term ***crappa*** meaning "chaff" (as in separate the wheat, the good stuff, from the chaff, the crap).

"Who reads this crap?"

Dritt (Norwegian) • Hovno (Czech) • Basura (Spanish)

For Fuck's Sake /four·fuhks·sakeh/

For when 'crikey' just won't cut it

1. an expression of anger, contempt, frustration

Swearing evolves to fit the needs of its society. Once upon a time, "For God's sake" did the job adequately and was all that was needed to calm the inner frustrations of a senseless world. In these modern, godless times, the phrase needed a reboot. We gave it a fuck and God said it was good.

"For fuck's sake, mate – give it a rest."

Porca Madonna (Italian)

Shite /schyte/

Shit done right – shite!

1. a foolish or deceitful person **2.** rubbish, nonsense

The Irish have always gone one better than the English and nowhere is that truer than with profanity. There is a joke about shite merely being the Irish misspelling shitty, but I'm not brave enough to write it. See also: gobshite.

"Guinness in London tastes like shite."

Merdique (French) • *Chujowy (Polish)*

Shit Off /schyt·orf/

Rarely used, but potent

1. a demand to leave **2.** a relatively soft and polite, and often affectionate, alternative to fuck off

Popularized for the first time in the brilliant sweary BBC TV show *The Thick of It*, which aired in 2006. It doesn't roll of the tongue as cleanly as "Fuck off!" but it cuts through better as a result.

"I don't mean to be rude, Geoff, but would you please just shit off."

DON'T FORGET: piss off, sod off, bugger off, cunt off

Up Yours /up·yawz/

Comes with a free two finger salute to boot!

1. a gesture of defiance **2.** a concluding message of departure **3.** an offer of extreme contempt

The phrase "Up Yours" (a contraction of "Up Your Bum" or "Up Your Ass" or "Shove It Up Your Own Ass") has a vague traceable history. Let's leave it at that. The most iconic (and baffling) usage of the phrase appeared in the film *Independence Day* just before the character shot, quite literally, a canon up an alien spaceship's rear opening.

"All right, you alien assholes! In the words of my generation: Up Yours!"
   Russell Casse

"Up yours, Daddy, this is my ice cream."

Que te folle un pez (Spanish) • *Vai para o caralho (Portuguese)*

Get Bent /get·bent/

Something for the straightlaced

1. an expression of defiance and displeasure

In mid-twentieth century US culture "Get Bent" was used as a hippie/beatnik phrase to insult straight, corporate types. In the UK, around the same time, it was employed as a dumb expression for dumb homophobes, as well relating to corruption ("Get bent, copper!") and getting one's knickers in a twist i.e. "Don't get bent out of shape."

Today, the phrase is seemingly detached from all its origins and simply a less polite alternative to "Go away" or "No way" or to express your no doubt deserved defiance.

"How much? You can get bent, mate."

Spierdalaj (Polish: Get the fuck away)

Piss Off /pis·orf/

Urine for a treat with this one

1. leave at once **2.** an expression of astonishment, confusion and/or rejection

Bodily fluids are common in profanity and piss certainly comes second only to, er, cum, by a whisker. Feeling **pissed** (drunk), **pissed off** (to be annoyed) and "Piss off" (go away) are all common piss-based profanity. "Piss off" first started circulating in Britain in the 1920s, while to "get pissed" dates back to the 1810s.

"Piss off 'mate' before I break your legs."

Faire chier (French)

Bloody Hell /blud·ee·hel/

An oldie but a goodie

1. an expression of surprise, frustration, disdain or contempt

A no-no in the eighteenth century when it was banned, the word bloody was once considered one of the most profane intensifiers. As an adjective it was first recorded in 1627 ("Bloody thief!") and as an adverb in 1676 ("Bloody drunk"). Today, in the UK, "Bloody Hell" is a mild invective, though the US still considers it relatively profane.

"Where the bloody hell am I?"

Cholera (Polish) • Svarte helvete (Norwegian) • Sanguinosa inferno (Italian)

Slut /sluht/

Sluts deserve celebrating, not shaming

1. a sexually promiscuous or uninhibited person
2. a disrespectable individual **3.** term of abuse

The word dates back to the fourteenth century. Everyone's favourite literary pervert, Geoffrey Chaucer, used it lovingly and the word has taken on many forms ever since. Samuel Johnson's famous first dictionary had room for "Slut", describing it as a "dirty woman". Interestingly enough, Johnson meant dirty in a non-sexual sense. Heslut can be used for men.

"John is such a slut – he must have gobbled a thousand fellas last night."

Ráicleach (Irish) • Yariman (Japanese) • Tua mamma bocchinara (Italian: 'Your Mum's a fluffer')

Prick /prik/

For when you feel a 'dick' is too soft to use…

1. a penis **2.** a person who acts like a penis (a despicable person)

As a euphemism for a penis, prick dates back to the 1500s. Shakespeare had Romeo's mate, Mercutio, deliver the line in *Romeo and Juliet* as clever wordplay. In recent years, prick has slid up and down the ranks of offensiveness. It is used more as a term of endearment these days.

"Oh Betty, you silly prick, you let you tea grow cold."

Jot (Korean) • Kutya faszát (Hungarian: Dog dick) • Vittu (Finnish) • Punzada (Spanish)

Minger /ming·uh/

Beauty is in the eye of the beerholder

1. an unattractive person **2.** a repulsive thing (minging)

Bint, hag, fugly – there are many profane invectives to describe an unsightly person or item. Urban Dictionary describes a minger rather gloriously: "Someone who was not just touched by the ugly stick at birth but was battered severely with it." Nuff said.

"See that man at the bar – proper minger."

Busu (Japanese) • *Mota kutta (Hindi: Fat dog)* • *Grim (Danish)*

Jesus Fucking Christ
/ge·zuss·fuhk·kuhng·kraist/

OMG it's JFC!

1. an exhalted exsparation and exclamation of surprise, wonder, shock, disappointment, frustration

You're going to a special place in Hell for buying this book. But for this swear word in particular s seat will be reserved with your name on. Jesus Fucking Christ!, or simply Jesus Christ!, if you're in a rush to take the Lord's name in vain, has been a favourite blaspheme since, well, the dawn of time, quite literally, the year 0, when Christ was born. Its divine usage in popular culture is so prevalent it's probably the reason why Jesus hasn't come back to save us again.

"Jesus titty-fucking Christ, Carl, that shart stank."

Holy Shit /how·lee·schyt/

Welcome to the worst curse on earth…

1. an expression of awe, surprise, astonishment, fear, disappointment

Much of profanity's continued success is down to the intensifier that comes before or after the swear word. Holy shit is fun because its sacrilegious without even trying to be. The intensifier originated from phrases such as "Holy Moses" and "Holy Mary Mother of God" and "Holy Tintinnabulation Batman!".

"Holy shit! I just saw a man fall down a well."

Puta que pariu (Portuguese) • *Wǒ Cào (Chinese)*

Dotard /doh·tud/

In a nutshell, Donald Trump

1. a physically weak and/or mentally diminished old person

Dotard dates back to 1350 Middle English era, combining "dote" (a foolish simpleton) with -"ard", a pejorative suffix in common nouns such as bastard, coward, drunkward, retard, etc.

"Action is the best option in treating the dotard who, hard of hearing, is uttering only what he wants to say."

Kim Jong-un, 2017 (about Donald Trump)

Radoteur (French) • Bacucco (Italian)

Mugwump /muhg·wumph/

Our new favourite invective

1. a person who believes they are superior
2. aloofness **3.** a general term of abuse

Somewhat ironically, before British Prime Minister Boris Johnson used the word 'Mugwump' to describe Jeremy Corbyn, his opposition counterpart, during the general election campaign of 2019, the word hadn't been used as an insult in decades. Its original meaning was someone who is superior or aloof. Now, it's taken on a new life of its own and mugwump has now become one of the most obscene words in the English language, a sort of beefed-up version of the slang word "mug" ("Don't mug me off, mate, or I'll break your face" or "You're a mug for voting for Boris Johnson."

"Jeremy Corbyn is a mutton-headed old mugwump."
   Boris Johnson

Douche /doosh/

Hugely popular catch-all insult

1. an obnoxious or unlikeable person (you know quite a few)

Douche, and its accessorized counterpart, douchebag, have been named "the ultimate slur against privileged white men". While "douche" began as a French word meaning "a jet of water flushed into the vagina in order to wash it or treat it medically", the word has become wildly popular in the US. So, how one became the other will remain another of life's greatest curiosities.

"DJ is such a douche for spoiling the ending of *The Sixth Sense*."

Duschen (German)

$#@!

CHAPTER
TWO

CONTEMPORARY
SWEARING

"Swearing was invented as a
compromise between running
away and fighting."

Peter Finley Dunne

Shit the Bed /schyt·the·bed/

For when the shit really hits the skids…

1. to fail beyond words **2.** an exclamation that expresses surprise

Historians have really shit the bed on defining the history of this phrase. However, when humans die, they tend to shit the bed, quite literally, so let's say that's the origin of this one…

"John shit the bed when he died."

Scheiße aufs bett (German) • ¡Me cago en la leche! (Spanish: I shit in the milk)

DON'T FORGET: fucked up, clusterfuck, screwed the pooch

Dickasaurus /dik·a·saw·rus/

Dicks come in all shapes and sizes… and dinosaur species

1. a person who screws up **2.** a big dick (literally and figuratively)

Despite dinosaurs having been dead for 65 million years, dickasaurus is a relativity new piece of profanity, originating via the late twentieth century with the arrival of Internet-based "franken-swears" – i.e. two swear words stuck together to form a super swear. Monty Python's Roman emperor, *Biggus Dickus*, is a close equivalent.

"I can't believe Tommy slept through his exam – what a dickasaurus!"

Arschgeige (German)

Asshat /aas·hat/

One size fits all

1. an obnoxious and ignorant person

Asshat derives from the visual metaphor, and popular slang expression, "To have one's head up one's ass" or, more colloquially, "get your head out of your ass!" The recipient is so clueless about an unfolding event that they must be blind from wearing their ass as a hat. The term "asshead" has been with us as an insult since 1541, when an English cleric named Thomas Becon wrote, "little pleasure have these **asse heades** in hearing the glorious and blessed word of God."

"Dave, you asshat! We've run out of beer."

Arschgesicht (German) • Skitstövel! (Swedish: Shit-boot)

 **DON'T FORGET:** asshole, asshelmet, assclown, assmuncher, asspirate, asswipe, assmonkey, assgoblin; UK – replace all with arse

Choad /chode/

Remember: choads are neither big nor clever

1. a penis that is as short as it is fat **2.** to behave like an embarrassing dick

A variant of the word **choda** (penis), which derives from **chodna**, a Hindi word meaning 'to excite'. Pencil-dick, babycock, CD (compact dick), microschlong – all variations on a theme that will do the job nicely.

"My brother's acting like an absolute choad today."

"I can't work with a choad."

Micropene (Spanish) • Un petit penis (French) • Kleinpenis (German: No dick) • Koki (Hungarian)

Douche Canoe /doosh-kanoo/

When douche just won't do

1. a person who exceeds the limits of being a normal douche or douchebag

The word "douche" derives from the French term "Douche", meaning a shower of water. Canoes, obviously, work best on water. Douche Nozzle is also popular (for the same reason).

"Homework on a weekend? My teacher is such a douche canoe."

Gilipollas (Spanish)

Shitgibbon /schyt·gibb·on/

Be gentle to gibbons

1. a person who has greatly displeased another
2. a term of abuse

Shitgibbon has been traced back to the early 1990s when comedy writer David Quantick employed it in an issue of music magazine *NME*. It has been credited to the writer ever since, and recently found fame in the US via the TV show *Veep*, which Quantick also wrote for.

"Donald Trump is a tiny-fingered, Cheeto-faced, ferret-wearing shitgibbon."

Bitchtits /bich·titz/

"This is Bob. Bob has bitchtits." Fight Club

1. a man with man-boobs **2.** a term of abuse

"Bitch" has long been a derogatory way of referring to a woman and it remains an all-too-common swear in that singular sense. Bitchtits, however, is a term of abuse for men who own or develop breasts, perhaps due to drinking too much white wine, and/or ingesting way too many steroids, or regrettably have a rare, but life-threatening, illness. The slang has also slipped into general usage to mean anything insulting towards a man's appearance.

"Is it just me or has Phil put on weight? Are those bitchtits."

Salope-les-seins (French) • Nyeon (Korean)

Cockplonker /kok·plong·kuh/

A penetrative contraction contraption

1. a person who plonks on top of a penis **2.** an incompetent person **3.** something large

The first use of plonker to mean a "wally" is believed to have been in a 1981 episode of *Only Fools and Horses*. It became a definitive article of London East End slang. A cockplonker, well, you can figure it out.

"Rodney, you plonker!"

"Son, stop pulling your plonker and help me clean the car."

Verga (Spanish) • *Casa do caralho (Portuguese: House of the dick)*

Buswanker

Buswanker /buhs·wang·kuh/

Best said as one word

1. a person, predominantly a "chav", who can't afford any means of transport except a bus **2.** a term of general abuse

Popularized in the first half of the noughties on *The Inbetweeners*, a hugely popular comedy show set around a bunch of unpopular, but lovable, sixth formers and the way they interact with each other. Today, the word has transcended its etymology and is used to describe any type of wanker, bus-based or otherwise.

"Rex and Mike are basically poor. Total buswankers!"

Shitshow /schyt·show/

If you're in the wrong place at the wrong time you know where you are

1. *Collins English Dictionary* satisfactorily sums this one up: "A chaotic, freewheeling state of affairs characterized by rampant disorder and the apparent absence of any thoughtful organization."

The word's possible provenance dates back to the 1974 *Yearbook of the European Convention of Human Rights*, where this phrase turned up: "We don't want this shit-show to go on any longer." Sadly, human rights are still a shitshow nearly fifty years later.

"What a shitshow Brexit was!"

Ah, jot-gat-ne (Korean)

DON'T FORGET: FUBAR (Fucked Up Beyond All Repair) and SNAFU (Situation Normal All Fucked Up)

Shitler /schyt·lur/

Hitler deserves this, to be fair

1. a nasty piece of shit **2.** a bad person **3.** a person who has done unspeakable shitty things

I'll assume you know who Adolf Hitler is. Add shit as a prefix to his name and, well, you get the picture. Shitbag is also a fun alternative, as is shitfuck.

"My boss made me stay late on Friday. Total shitler."

fuck-a-doodle-doo

Fuck-a-doodle-doo

/fuhk·a·doo·dul·doo/

For those who couldn't care less about giving a fuck

1. a sarcastic expression of uncaring and disinterest

Cockerels (the young male chickens) have been saying cock-a-doodle-do for thousands of years. It's arguably all they do. Anyway, it wasn't long before humans copied their clarion call. The phrase received recognition in the 2004 classic zombie film *Shaun of the Dead*. The US equivalent would be, like, "Whatever."

"You got a new haircut? Fuck-a-doodle-doo."

Tanto faz (Portuguese) • Peu importe (French)

Assclown /ass·klown/

The literal butt-end of the joke

1. a buffoon **2.** a joker **3.** an incompetent person

This delightfully sarcastic term of endearment was given to the world in the seminal work of Beavis & Butthead creator, Mike Judge, in his 1999 movie *Office Space*. Due to the then-cult, now-classic status of the movie, every quote has made its way into the mainstream and become an iconic phrase.

"Take your dick out of the mash potato – you assclown!"

Arschloch (German) • Estúpido (Spanish) • Testa di cazzo (Italian)

Buttplug /buht·pluhg/

Pucker up…it's about to get hairy

1. a device for anal play **2.** an incompetent, lame or obnoxious person

The sex toy known as a Buttplug was invented circa the 1890s and first sold as Dr Young's Ideal Rectal Dilator. Let's assume the insult "buttplug" was created the very moment the first sex toy was first sold – as the punishment fits the crime. For those who want to pretend they have no heavenly idea what a buttplug is, imagine this: it's a plug for your butt.

"Barry, don't be such a buttplug – we'll get you to hospital in time."

Plug anal (French)

Sascrotch /sa·skrotch/

The legend is real

1. an unpleasant penis **2.** a brutish man

In North American folklore, Sasquatch (also known as Bigfoot) are referred to as large, hirsute, bi-pedal, ape-like creatures that dwell in forest and mountain wildernesses. A sascroth is someone with (or behaves like) a big, hairy, smelly dick. The legendary film *Ron Burgundy Anchorman* famously gave rise to the phrase with the iconic quote, "It smells like Bigfoot's dick…" referring, of course, to Sex Panther, the male cologne that works "60 per cent of the time, all the time".

"Eugh, John, stop waving that sascrotch around – it stinks."

Affenschwanz (German: Apedick)

Cockwomble /kok·wom·bul/

You'll never think of the Wombles of Wimbledon in the same way again

1. a person who thinks they're better than everyone else **2.** an incompetent individual

Taking its origins from the idiom "Cock of the Walk" (someone who dominates others within a group), cockwomble is now one of the twenty-first century's most popular pieces of profanity. Not unsurprisingly, in 2018, at the height of the Brexit clusterfuck by British politicians, there were almost 70 Google searches a week for "cockwomble".

"Boris Johnson is an absolute cockwomble."

Fini à la pisse (French: Finished with piss – i.e. a person conceived with semen and urine)

Spunktrumpet /

spuhngk·truhm·puht/

Do you play?

1. a penis **2.** a dickish person

In recent years, spunktrumpet has become one of the nation's favourite new swear words. Why call someone a boring old "dick" when spunktrumpet is so much more – satisfying. I mean, just picture it in your mind now – a spunktrumpet. What do you see?

"Sandra's mum caught her playing on Billy's spunktrumpet last night."

Boludo (Argentian)

Shitflute /schyt·floot/

Pianos are much easier to play.

1. a sex act where a person performs oral sex on a penis after anal sex **2.** a despicable person

What was once an intimate moment between two consenting partners in the privacy of their own home has now become the rising star of profanity in the past few years. Naturally, the proliferation of hard-core pornography on the Internet is to blame. You'll never look at a flute the same way again, either.

"Dave is such a backstabbing shitflute!"

Rassgat (Icelandic)

wankpuffin

Wankpuffin /wahnk·puh·fn/

Poor, poor puffins...

1. a word to describe a pitiful and pathetic person

Wankpuffin became a big viral sensation in 2016 when a Twitter user tweeted that his elderly mother's ISP name was "Wankpuffin". Next thing you know, the word is everywhere. The fusion of "wank" and "puffin" (just a North Atlantic sea bird, remember) quickly became the go-to cock-based insult to describes general wankers, of which there are quite a few, sadly.

"Did you see Trump on TV last night – what a wankpuffin."

buttfugly

Buttfugly /buht·fuh·glee/

Three words for the price of one

1. a supremely unattractive person

Butt fucking ugly is quite a mouthful, so it's no wonder that it became smooshed down to one. The Internet reliably informs us that "fugly" has been around since the 1970s, and **fugh** has been an expression of revulsion or abhorrence since the 1680s. The word was famously used in the 2004 hit movie *Mean Girls*: "That girl is the nastiest skank bitch I've ever met. Do not trust her. She is a fugly slut."

"Your mama is so buttfugly her mirror turns away when she looks at it."

Laide (French) • Feo (Spanish)

CHAPTER
THREE

CRUDE
SWEARING

"A lot of people say that
it's a lack of vocabulary
that makes you swear. Rubbish.
I know thousands of words
but I still prefer 'fuck'."

Billy Connolly

Whorebag /haw·bag/

Not available to buy on eBay

1. an oversexed and sexually uninhibited person (someone who gives many fucks)

The word "whore" earned its leading letter "w" in 1535 when there is a record of the spelling change, from **hore**, though no evidence as to why that change occurred. The Old English word **hore**, meaning prostitute, has been in use since before 1100CE. The word "bag" implies a whore so large that within herself she could fit many other whores. Manwhore can also be applied to males.

"Judy fucked two guys last night – such a whorebag!"

Houra (Finnish) • Putain de salope (French: Whore of a whore) • Schlampe (German)

Twatbadger /twat·ba·juh/

Badgers – friend or foe? You decide

1. a black and white pubed vagina **2.** a stupid and detestable person

Twats and badgers go way back. For many gardeners they are one and the same thing – a pest. For others, twatbadgers are lovely to look at and feed every now again. As a general multi-purpose slang insult, twatbadger has been taken under the wing by millennials and hipsters below the age of 25.

"Her twatbadger wrinkled its nose at me it was so hungry for cock."

"Felix, you twatbadger, that's not how you drain a radiator."

Cocknose /kok·nowz/

Cock, meet Nose

1. a man with a large nose **2.** a man with a runny penis **3.** a general-purpose term of abuse

It makes sense that two of the body's largest extremities work well together as an insulting invective. "Big nose" has long been a lazy curse upon a person's person. Cocknose, however, goes straight for the jugular – the penis. Don't try and google "Cocknose images" FYI – you won't be able to unsee it.

"Oi, cocknose, move your head, I can't see the screen!"

Turdweasel!

Turdweasel /tuhd·wee·zl/

Shitweazel, fuckweasel, cockweasel – any weazel will do

1. a sneaky, shifty person with extra added shittiness **2.** an example of foul language

Not, as you might think, the turd droppings of a weasel. Instead, a turdweasel is reserved for that special brand of person who, say, never pays for a taxi, or forgets their wallet on a night out. A Turdfuck will work equally as well.

"It's your turn to buy a drink, you cheap turdweasel."

Grundlemuncher

/grun·dul·munh·chuh/

Not one of Lewis Carroll's nonsense words

1. a person who takes enjoyment from snacking on a perineum

Grundle, gooch, taint – it doesn't matter what you call it, it's still that sweaty smelly zone between the back of your balls and your butthole. The doctor's call it your perineum – the prudes!

"Carol, she used to be a proper grundlemuncher before she married Kevin."

DON'T FORGET: Bandersnatch (one of Lewis Carroll's), vajayjay, fanny, cooch, bajingo, foof, fadge, ham sandwich, beef curtains, badly packed kebab, moose knuckle, wizard's sleeve, donkey's yawn. I could go on…

Tainttickler /teint·ti·kuh·luh

It's called a taint because t'aint your balls and t'aint your ass

1. the growth of facial hair directly beneath a man's lower lip (also known as a soul patch.)
2. a term of endearment **3.** a person who is sexually uninhibited **4.** a term of gross abuse

That sweet spot – well, actually, it tastes more salty – between the genitals and bumhole is called a taint. A tainttickler, therefore, is a brave and adventurous person willing to get up close and personal with that part of a body and use their facial hair (doesn't have to be a man) to tickle that spot until its slippery and wet.

"I hear Jodie's new man is a bit of a tainttickler."

Shitcunt /schyt·kuhnt/

Welcome to the worst curse on earth...

1. the lowest and, paradoxically, highest level of cunt you can achieve

A shitcunt is a very bad thing. It's not a term reserved for people who are bad at being cunts, it's a term for cunts who *excel* at being cunts, the shittiest of all cunts, in fact. The Internet says it originated in Australia, which sounds about right (just kidding).

"Why did you throw my car keys down the drain, you shitcunt?"

Cocainus /kow·kein·nuhs/

Don't get high on your own supply

1. a smug, confident and arrogant arsehole high on cocaine **2.** name-calling for junkies

The history of the drug cocaine is littered with the husks of people who have disappeared up their own ass. The term "cocainus" is still relatively new in the lexicon; it's waiting for that special asshole to come along and define it. My money's on <deleted for legal reasons>.

"Did you see that guy last night – total cocainus."

Hok a chanik (Yiddish: Forever talking nonsense)

GIMPAZOID

Gimpazoid /gimp·a·zoyd/

Part-robot, part-man, part-gimp

1. a person who is considered pathetic, embarrassing and/or silly

Humans are close to becoming the first, and only, species on earth able to make love to a computer or some form of AI humanoid. The origin of "gimp" derives from a sexual fetishist who likes to be dominated, most often while dressed in a rubber body suit complete with mask, zips and chains. A gimpazoid is a robot-controlled gimp, I guess. As a metaphor, gimpazoid's popularity as a profanity has increased in tandem with the human race's impending slavery to the machines. We'll all be gimpazoids soon.

"Don't call my mum hot, Donny, you gimpazoid!"

Schlump (Yiddish)

Choadgobbler /chode·gob·bleugh/

Cockgoblin, if you prefer

1. a person who enjoys small penises or oral fixation **2.** a term of invective to define a lame or loathsome individual

The paradox of this profanity is that to gobble a choad (a penis as short as it is wide) would mean to either purse your lips together or open your mouth very wide, depending on the penis size and shape. Not to be confused with "floppy gobbler": a person who enjoys gobbling the hood of a woman's clitoris. I'm not making these up, I promise.

"Lucy choadgobbled Ben last night – it wasn't pretty apparently."

Jizzwipe /jiz·waip/

A sock, towel, the curtains, a crisp packet, oven mitt, your partner's mouth, anything, really, that can be used to deposit your man goo

1. a "fuck cloth" used to entrap semen following ejaculation   **2.** a useless or ineffectual person so crap that they resemble a garment loaded with jizz

Until someone actually invents a proper "jizzcloth", a piece of fabric specifically – scientifically – designed to clean up ejaculate, men will continue to wipe their "jizz" willy-nilly any place they feel will complete the job. As a term of abuse, rather aptly, the word is used to describe someone who needs to pull their finger out and stop acting like a marzipan dildo i.e. get the job done. A jizztard, jizzock, jizzass, or jizzbitch, is also applicable.

"Jesus, Tom, don't be such a lazy jizzwipe."

Serviette de sperme (French)

Shitbiscuit /schyt·bi·skuht/

Not the champion thoroughbred horse (that's Seabiscuit)

1. an expression of shock or surprise **2.** an idiotic or incompetent person **3.** an unfortunate situation or event

Contracted from the visually awesome metaphor "shit on a biscuit!" (to be surprised), shitbiscuit now is predominantly is related to a stupid person who has acted within the limits of their inherent nature.

"What the shitbiscuit is James banging on about?"

Na mou klaseis ta'rxidia (Greek: Fart on my balls)

Dildo /dil·dow/

You put the pink one in, you pull the white one out, in out, in out, shake it all about

1. a non-vibrating rubber sex toy for insertion into bodily orifices **2.** a woeful and absurd person

Humans have been using (stone) dildos for 30,000 years. That's a fact. Look it up if you don't believe me. The term "dildo", however, was first used around 1400, originating from the Latin **dilatare** ('open wide!'), and the Italian **diletto**, which means 'delight'. Rubber dildos are used now – so much easier to wipe clean.

"Janice, don't just stand there like a dildo, help me get the bags out of the car."

Robertek (Czech) • Plastikschwanz (German) • Godemiché (French)

Clunge /kluhnj/

Do you dare take the plunge?

1. a well-lubricated vagina **2.** an obtuse person

The word clunge has its origins in British TV sitcoms of the 1970s, where it was used to mean "arse", and in 2008, on *The Inbetweeners*, it jumped gender entirely meaning a female vagina, no doubt thanks to its apt use of a hard consonant opening (cl–) and soft and moist (-unge) ending.

"I love a good wet clunge. Don't you, Grandma?"

Fisse (Danish) • Le chatte (French)

Wanker /wahn·ker/

Would a wanker by any other name smell as sweet?

1. a person loyal to masturbation **2**. a person who acts improper

This beautiful bit of British slang, originating from the word "wank" (to masturbate), has no lineage, but is believed to date back to the 1940s. A recent study by leading British broadcasting organizations revealed that the word "wanker" was the fourth most offensive word in the UK – after cunt, motherfucker and fuck.

"Don't go home yet, you wanker. Stay for another drink."

Wichser (German) • Branleur (French) • Segaiolo (Italian)

Twat /twat/

'Tis not twot

1. a vulva **2.** an expression of anger **3.** an obnoxious person

Twat dates back to 1650 and takes its name from an old Norse word, **thveit**, which meant a slit or cut. (Hence the vulva connection – great name for a band, incidentally.) Americans are unable to say twat so, rather annoyingly, they say twot. Which it is not.

"Don't act like a twat, son."

Hùn zhàng (Chinese) • Fotze (German) • Coglione (Italian)

Dickfuck /dik·fuhk/

If you're going to give a fuck, make it this one

1. an unparalleled moron

Any profanity suffixed with fuck is absolutely unbeatable in a battle of wits. Ratfuck, twatfuck, cuntfuck, fatfuck, thinfuck, bigfuck, smallfuck – you get the picture.

"What have you done, you dickfuck?"

Cazzo (Italian) • Caralho (Portuguese) • Poshol na khui: (Russian: Go ride a dick)

Bumder /buhm·dur/

Bummer meet Bender

1. a derogatory term for a heterosexual person
2. a general term of abuse

Another phrase that became popular due to its placement on the *The Inbetweeners*. Today, "bumder" has transcended its origin (and very offensive) meaning and is applied quite commonly as a general term of affectionate banter between people you would consider "lads".

"Oi, bumder, piss off!"

Fucktastic /fuhk·tazztik/

Fantastic – but way, way fucking better

1. an indescribable sexual feeling **2.** a highly skilled sexual performer **3.** a good thing

The word fantastic comes from the Latin ***phantasticus***, meaning "imaginary". It's been around since the fourteenth century. Fucktastic is a relatively new portmanteau, becoming popularized around the late 1990s, following the birth of Internet technologies, and the proliferation of profanity.

"Paul is super-fucktastic in the bedroom. Highly recommended."

Dickhead /dik·hed/

Classic slang… from tip to base

1. an irritating and/or annoying person

As you're fully aware by now, there is a plethora of penis-based euphemisms out in the wild – dickbag, dickhole, bellend, knobhead, nobbag, dickwad, etc. But dickhead is the perennially popular profanity that's good for all weather. The etymology of the term used to describe a penis belongs to the early 1890s when it was first recorded in a farmer's slang dictionary. However, the story of Dick Whittington has been around since the fourteenth century, so it's possible "dick" was used as an insult before that.

"Use your brains – don't be a dickhead."

"You don't know dick about how to fix a washing machine."

Cúl tóna (Irish) • Arschgeige (German)

Shitfaced /schyt·feist/

Drunk has many levels but this is the best

1. supremely and extremely intoxicated on alcohol or drugs (often both if you've got a good dealer)

As long as shit has been hitting the fan it's been flying into people's faces. One of the earliest mentions of being **chit-faced** can be found in Thomas Dekker's 1622 play *The Virgin Martyr*. Cunted also paints the same picture.

"I was beyond shitfaced at Jennie's wedding."

¡Me cago en la leche! (Spanish: I shit in the milk) • Quebrar (Spanish) • Plein comme un tonneau (French: Full like a barrel) • Aspackad (Swedish) • Kee maw (Thai)

Bullshit /bul·schyt/

Two syllables of glorious magnificence

1. unacceptable behaviour **2.** an expression of disbelief **3.** no fucking way **4.** a male cow's fecal waste

"Bull" has been employed to mean a lie or a falsehood since the old French word **bole**, which meant "deception", in the fourteenth century. It became popular slang in the US following the T.S. Eliot poem called *The Triumph of Bullshit*, which was written circa 1910.

"Donald Trump is talking some next-level bullshit."

Tull (Norweigian) • C'est des conneries (French) • Cazzate (Italian)

Pussy /pus·see/

Feline good

1. female genitalia **2.** a weak and cowardly person
3. the pet name for a domestic cat

The word "pussy" has related to any creature soft and furry for centuries, with the original purpose of "being catlike" perhaps emerging with the phrase "pussy-footed". Despite what President Donald Trump says, pussies of all varieties are not meant to be grabbed.

"Don't be scared of the dark, son, nobody likes a pussy."

Foufoune (French) • Mammoletta (Italian)

Bollocks /bo·luhks/

Never mind

1. testicles **2.** an exclamation to express dishonesty, disagreement or nonsense

Ballbags, nutsacks, gonads – whatever you call those dangly flapsacks of yours – have long been the fascination of human beings. And deservedly so, they're fucking weird. "Bollocks" derives from a word of Germanic origin, **ballock**, which obviously relates to that round-shaped object footballers kick about, as well the two spheres that dangle and swing perilously between your grundle and your asshole.

"I'm not getting in a car with you – bollocks to that!"

Cojones (Spanish) • Testicoli (Italian) • Les boules (French)

CHAPTER
FOUR

COMPULSIVE SWEARING

"Profanity provides relief
denied even to prayer."

Mark Twain

Fuck Off /fuhk·orf/

The G.O.A.T.

1. please leave immediately from the vicinity **2.** an expression of complete surprise and/or contempt

"Fuck Off", and its wonderful brother from the same mother "Fuck You", were said 0.3 seconds after the invention of the word "Fuck". Nothing clears the throat better…except maybe "Get fucked…"

"You can fuck off, mate, if you think I'm doing that."

Vaffanculo (Italian) • Váyase a la mierda (Spanish) • Verpiss Dich! (German) • Gae-sae (Korean) Kon da ti go natrese (Cantonese: get fucked by a horse)

Twunt /tw·unt/

A little bit of both goes a long way

1. a portmanteau of twat and cunt **2.** a despicable human being (Think: Nigel Farage)

Both "twat" and "cunt" were considered obscene by the mid-seventeenth century, but it's hard to say which particular genius decided to first squeeze them together. Shakespeare was rather fond of cunt, and loved inventing new words, so let's give him the credit/blame.

    Hamlet: "Lady, shall I lie in your lap?"
    Ophelia: "No, my lord."
    Hamlet: "Do you think I meant count-ry matters?"

"I was absolutely twunted the other night"

"Oi, don't be a twunt!"

Chatte (French) • Boceta (Portuguese)

Dumbfuck /duhm·fuhk/

When you can't see the forest for the trees…

1. an extraordinarily stupid person

The precise provenance of dumbfuck is hard to trace but dumbfucks have been doing dumbfuckery since the dawn of time, that much is self-evident. Today, the word dumb relates more to a lack of intelligence than it does to its Old English original meaning of "mute" or "unable to speak". The curse may have arisen from the word "dumbfounded", meaning greatly astonished or amazed.

"You can't park there – you dumbfuck."

Tonto/Tonta (Spanish)

Cunt /kuhnt/

What we've all been waiting for. The worst curse?

1. a vulgar word for a vagina **2.** not a term of endearment

Used as a term of abuse since the early nineteenth century, cunt actually found its origins in a London street name, Gropecunt Lane, believe it or not, circa 1230. There were many streets of this name around the UK at the time. Unsuprisingly, the streets were famed for their organized prostitution. The street names were changed to protect their identities.

"Jamie – he's a right proper cunt."

Aiteann (Irish) • Coño (Spanish) • Connard (French) • Fotze (German)

Retard /ree·taard/

Don't hoist yourself with your own retard

1. a mentally slow person **2.** a moron

How ironic that the word retard is French (just kidding!) derived from the word **retarder**, from the Latin **retardare**, meaning "back" + **tardus** "slow". The prefix re- can be seen in rewind, recycle, reuse, redo, etc. Historians have traced the word as far back as 1426. The first time the word "retard" was printed in American newspapers was in 1704. Today, the word is considered most rude for its ridicule of the mentally disabled, but it has also become a general-purpose profanity aimed at anyone whose behaviour is stupid or foolish.

"Booze makes Bob retarded."

Mogool (Dutch) • Perecear (Spanish)

DON'T FORGET: dummy, idiot, moron, imbecile, fool, dunce, ignoramus, fuckwit

Cuntychops /kuhntee·chops/

A friendlier and more affectionate version of "cunt"

1. would you believe; a term of endearment

Replacing the tough, clipped, hard-sounding double consonants and guttural stop of cunt with a friendly "y" (suggesting your insult is aimed at someone who is cunt-esque, and not a right proper cunt) and suffixing it with the word "chops" give this piece of profanity a much more affectionate ring to it. Effectively, "cuntychops" means "you're a slice of a cunt – not a whole one." Scottish in origin, naturally.

"Look at ol' cuntychops over there – he's a right mess."

Fucking Hell /fuhk·kunhg·hell/

Nothing says how you feel better than this

1. an expression of utter and unconsolable disbelief

As the great Billy Connolly said, "I'll stop saying 'Fucking hell' when somebody comes up with something better."

"I've got to look after the kids all day. I know, right, I'm like fucking hell!"

Téigh go dtí ifreann! (Irish) • *Create putain de merde (French)* • *Zur Hölle mit ihnen! (German)* • *Zajebiste (Polish: fucking awesome)* • *Helvetti (Swedish)*

Thundercunt /thuhn·duh·kuhnt/

Thunder, thunder, thunder, thunder... cunt!

1. a legendarily terrible person – a god among cunts

Urban Dictionary says it best: "Thundercunt is a term used to describe a person who is acting like such a cunt, that they alter the Earth's meteorological behaviour, resulting in near-apocalyptic storms with lethal levels of thunder. This is the worst level of cunt you can get." Clustercunt is also fun to say.

"The person who posted a wet slice of pizza through my letterbox last night is a right thundercunt."

Himmeldonnerwetter (German)

Fuckwit /fuhk·whit/

If you're dumber than fuck, welcome to the fuckwit club

1. a person who has no idea what a clue looks like

This vulgar slang was born and bred Australia. (I refuse to insert a joke about Australia being the home of the fuckwit.) The word's history goes back to the early 1970s. Fuckstick also has legs.

"Donald, get your head out of your arse and stop being such a fuckwit."

Gobdaw (Irish) • Teezak hamra (Arabic) • Idiota (Italian)

Smunt /smuhnt/

The worst type of cunt – a smug one

1. an arrogant and unpleasant person

Cunts, by their very nature, are the type of people who will be smug about being a cunt. Smunt is still in its infancy as a swear word – it's another franken-swear made up by computer nerds in the Internet age – and is often jettisoned in favour of its parent word, which, let's face it, is unbeatable. To be *smunted* is to be a smug cunt while shitfaced drunk.

"After she kissed that boy, Donna was such a smunt."

Go Fuck Yourself

/go·fuhk·yaw·self/

Don't just merely fuck off – go fuck yourself

1. an expression of incredulity and surprise **2.** a request to vacate your immediate surroundings

According to legend, in 1837, a woman was charged with obscenity after telling a group to "go fuck themselves", the first recorded usage of the phrase. Martin Scorsese's *Goodfellas* nailed it:

Spider: "Why don't you go fuck yourself, Tommy."
Tommy: *Shoots Spider.*

"Steve, go fuck yourself in the ass."

Gay kocken offen yom (Yiddish: Go shit in the ocean) •
Hoppaðu upp í rassgatið á þér (Icelandic: Hop up your own ass)
• *Va te faire foutre (French)*

Pissflap(s) /pis·flapp(s)/

It was this or pizzwizard

1. a lady's labium **2.** an obnoxious person **3.** an affectionate term of endearment for a close friend

In the box office smash of 2019 *Bohemian Rhapsody*, a pissed-up Freddie Mercury (played by Rami Malek, who won an Oscar for his portrayal of the singer) shouts to his passenger, "Get out of the car, you treacherous pissflap." The word has been trending, quite rightly so, ever since. Have you said it today?

"Oi, pissflap, shut your cakehole."

Zero Fucks Given
/zeeuh·row·fuhks·gi·vn/

Care less than anyone else…

1. 100 per cent indifference **2.** the inability to give even one fuck about someone or something

Not giving a fuck is fine, but it still sounds like you have at least one fuck to give. Eliminate that doubt and offer precisely zero fucks. This nifty little phrase was born in the late twentieth century, the lusty offspring of that old chestnut, "Couldn't give a flying fuck" and its many variants.

"My boss gave me a warning for being late today. Zero fucks given."

Je m'en fous (French)

Shut the Fuck Up
/shuht·thuh·fuhk·up/

STFU, for those who love acronyms

1. be quiet for fuck's sake

The use of the phrase "shut up" to mean "hold one's tongue" or "compel silence" dates back to the sixteenth century. Shakespeare used it in *King Lear*, don't you know. Shame he didn't add a fuck in there, though, that would have been cool.

"Shut the fuck up – I'm trying to watch the movie."

Por qué no te callas (Spanish) • *Qù nǐ de (Chinese)*

DON'T FORGET: cowfucker, deerfucker, bearfucker, goatfucker, sheepfucker, etc.

What the Fuck? /wot·the·fuhk/

WTF, am I right?

1. a rheretorical expression of disappointment, surprise and anger

Taking its origin from phrases such as "What the hell?", "What on earth?", "What the fuck?" has become popularized in the past decade as the computer-language acronym WTF, itself dating back as far as the mid-1980s and found to be a common curse for computer programmers when porn took too long to load.

"WTF, Susan? I was watching that."

Sjutton också (Swedish) • *Che cazzo (Italian: What the cock!)*

FYI (Fuck You, Idiot)

/fuhk·yoo·i·dee·uht/

Just For Your Information

1. a sarcastic adjustment of the email/social media acronyms FYI **2.** an expression of derision and disregard

FYI is used in more than three billion pointless emails sent every fucking day.

"You spilled your own pint – fuck you, idiot!"

Kutabare, boke (Japanese) • Küss meinen arsch (German: Kiss my ass) • Chupa-mos (Portuguese: Suck-it) • Sshi-bang-sae (Korean) • Kisama (Japanese) • Tsao ni zhu zhong shi ba dai (Mandarin: Fuck all your family)

DON'T FORGET: FML (Fuck My Life), LOL (Lots Of Load), LMAO (Laughing My Asshole Off), DTF (Down To Fuck), DGAF (Don't Give A Fuck) and PTFO (Passed The Fuck Out)

Bunglecunt /Buhng·gl·kuhnt/

Rolls off the tongue.

1. a person who tries hard to be a cunt but fails

2. a multipurpose term of name-calling

Bunglecunt has reached cultural saturation within the past few years, again no doubt due to the soft consonant of bungle gentrifying the hard consonants present within cunt. The origin of the word is unknown but shares similar letter arrangement to **bumbaclot**, a Jamaican slang equivalent to "motherfucker" often used as an interjection to express disgust.

"Richard is bunglecunting all over the place at the moment."

OMFG (Oh-My-Fucking-God)
/o·mi·fuhk·khung·god/

Forgive me father for I have OMFG'd

1. an exclamation of surprise or indignation

Religious fundamentalists will ask you politely to use the formal version of this invective – 'Oh My Fucking Good God'. But who has the time? Actually, religious extremists would probably prefer you say OML (Oh My Lord) instead of FML (Fuck My Lord) but you should never negotiate with terrorists.

"OMFG, Danny, STFU!"

Khange khodah (Farsi)

Cuntpuddle /kuhnt·puh·dl/

All the rage with Gen X, apparently

1. a woman who becomes so highly aroused that ejaculate pools around her feet **2.** a top-level bastard

A puddle is a wonderful noun to suffix with cunts. In one fell swoop the word conjures up a deep, wet and, perhaps, slightly stagnant and dirty location. Sure, you can have a cuntbath, cuntpool, cuntsea, cuntcanal, cuntgeyser, cuntcreek, cuntlagoon, cuntswamp and even cuntalluvial fan, but none of them are as satisfying as cuntpuddle.

"My cuntpuddle was so big after watching *Magic Mike* at the cinema, I had to put a binbag down."

DON'T FORGET: nonsense, horseshit, dogshit, codswallop, hogcock

Motherfucker /muh·thuh·fuh·kuh/

When you absolutely, positively, have to insult every last motherfucker in the room, accept no substitutes

1. a lousy excuse of a person **2.** mother-based lovemaker **3.** a difficult task

The history of this word is a motherfucker to work out. Read Sigmund Freud's *Interpretation of Dreams* (1899) and his analysis of the Oedipal Complex for more details. Strangely, fatherfucker just doesn't have quite the same ring to it.

"That exam was a motherfucker."

"You God-damn lying motherfuckin' son-of-a-bitch."

Fill de puta (Spanish) • Kusottare (Japanese) • Jebiesz jeze (Polish: you fuck hedgehogs) • Mang/pong (Thai: Your mother/your father!) • Ihre mutter säugt schweine (German: Your mother suckles swine)

Piece of Shit /pee·suv·schyt/

A slice of shit – not quite as shitty as a whole shit

1. an untrustworthy or loathsome person **2.** an item of poor quality

Sure, you can say a "piece of cock" or "piece of fuck" but it just doesn't work as well. Perhaps the greatest and most iconic use of this phrase came in Adam Sandler's classic movie *Happy Gilmore*:

Shoot McGavin: "You're in trouble, pal. I eat pieces of shit like you for breakfast."

Happy Gilmore: "You eat pieces of shit for breakfast?"

"That movie was a worthless piece of shit!"

Scheißkopf (German: Shithead) • *Monte de merda (Portugese)* • *Espèce de grosse merde (French)*

Clusterfuck /klus·ta·fak/

Fucked up beyond all repair

1. a calamitous mishandling of a situation

This was originally derived from a US military term, "Charlie Foxtrot", to refer to multiple failings within a single incident.

"That project was a complete clusterfuck from base to tip."

Gigantisk fuck-up (Norwegian) • Ah, jot-gat-ne (Korean)

DON'T FORGET: omnishambles, SNAFU, megabodge, bollocks-up, bungle